STEM

Living with Type 1 Diabetes

Understanding Ratios

Nicole Sipe

Contributing Author

Alison S. Marzocchi, Ph.D.

Consultant

Samantha Thompson, R.D., C.D.E.
Diabetes Educator

Colleen Pollitt, M.A.Ed.
Math Support Teacher
Howard County Public Schools

Publishing Credits

Rachelle Cracchiolo, M.S.Ed., *Publisher*
Conni Medina, M.A.Ed., *Editor in Chief*
Dona Herweck Rice, *Series Developer*
Emily R. Smith, M.A.Ed., *Series Developer*
Diana Kenney, M.A.Ed., NBCT, *Content Director*
Stacy Monsman, M.A., *Editor*
Michelle Jovin, M.A., *Associate Editor*
Fabiola Sepulveda, *Graphic Designer*

Image Credits: p.9 (bottom) Astrid & Hanns-Frieder Michler/Science Source; p.19 (top) BSIP SA/Alamy; p.24 (left) Jonathan Ernst/Reuters/Newscom; p.25 Dennis Van Tine/ABACAUSA.COM/Newscom; p.26 (left) Mitch Gunn/Shutterstock; p.27 Gabi De Morais/Shutterstock; all other images from iStock and/or Shutterstock.

Teacher Created Materials
5301 Oceanus Drive
Huntington Beach, CA 92649-1030
www.tcmpub.com

ISBN 978-1-4258-5879-7

Printed in Malaysia
Thumbprints.21254

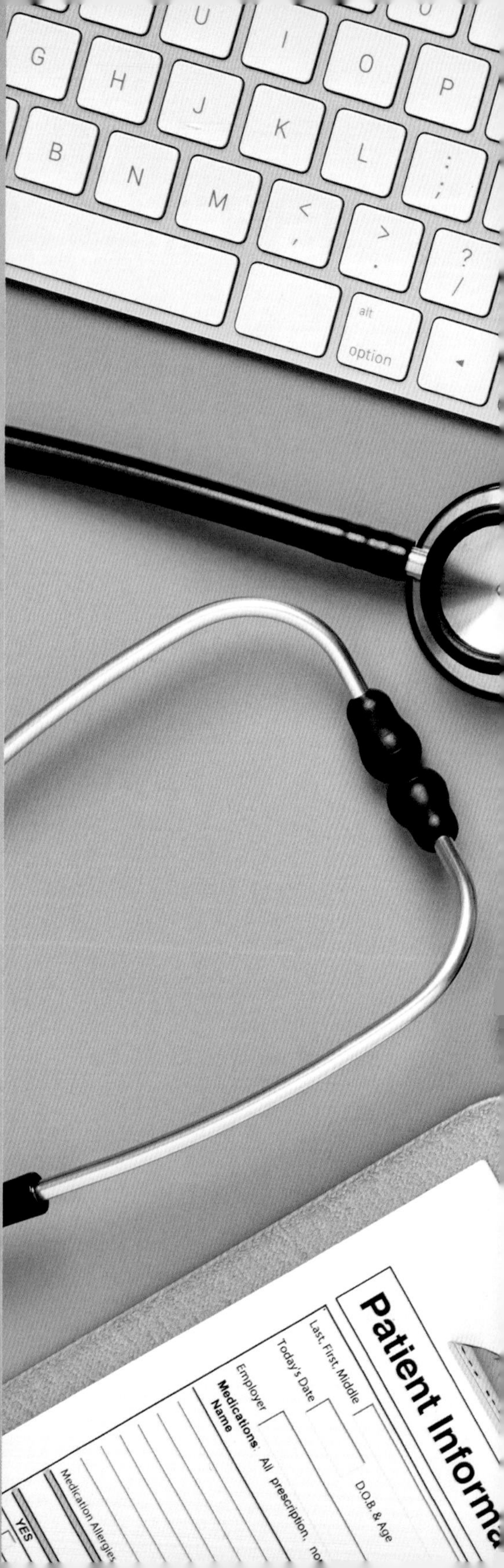

Table of Contents

A Different Normal

It's lunchtime at school and you're starving. Today is pizza day in the cafeteria—your favorite day! The spicy smell wafts down the hall and makes your mouth water. Your stomach grumbles, and you can almost swear it's saying, "Feed me now!" You can't wait to take a bite of a hot, cheesy, pepperoni-studded slice.

You and your friends amble toward the cafeteria, and they make a left at the fork in the hall to go toward it. Ignoring your grumbling stomach for a moment, you make a right toward the nurse's office. A visit to the school nurse before lunch is a normal part of your lunchtime routine.

The nurse greets you like always and has your supplies ready. You've done this a hundred (probably a thousand, feels like a million) times before. She knows the drill and so do you.

Before you found out you had Type 1 diabetes, you used to be afraid of needles. The thought of someone poking and prodding you sent a cold chill down your spine. Now, giving yourself injections of life-saving **insulin** at mealtimes has become a commonplace task. It is something you do every day, multiple times a day, and it is part of your life. It's normal for you. A *different* normal, yes—but it's *your* normal.

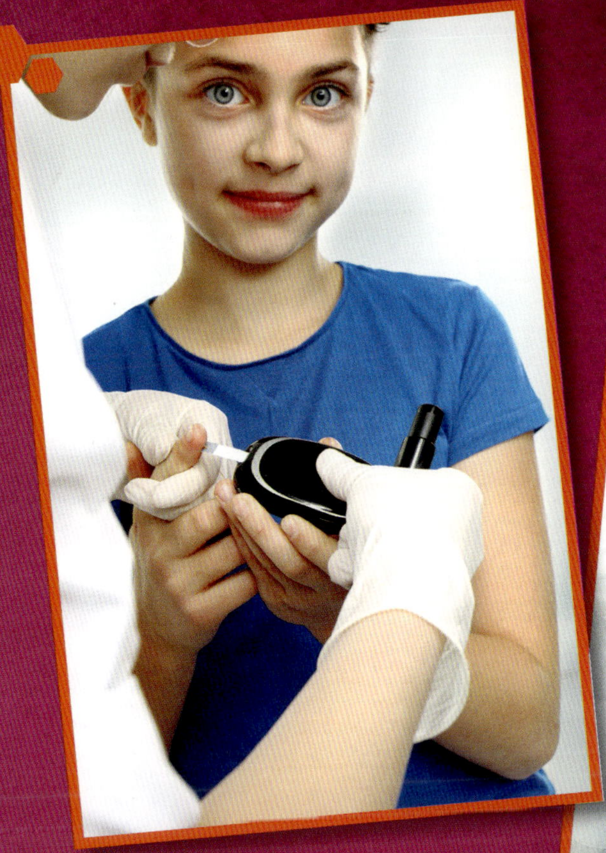

LET'S EXPLORE MATH

At lunchtime, 3 students visit the nurse to have their blood sugar levels checked, and 9 students visit the nurse to have their temperatures checked.

1. Choose all the correct ratios of students getting their blood sugar levels checked to students having their temperatures checked.

   A. 3:9

   B. 9:3

   C. 3:1

   D. 1:3

2. After helping the students, the nurse records $\frac{3}{12}$ in the daily report. What does this mean?

What Is Type 1 Diabetes?

Type 1 diabetes is an **autoimmune disease** that prevents the body from getting energy from food. Behind your stomach, sits a gland called the **pancreas** (PAN-kree-uhs). This flat gland is in charge of making a **hormone** called insulin. Insulin is what helps turn sugar and other food into energy. People's bodies naturally release insulin when they eat. Insulin helps sugars from food enter the body's cells to be used for energy.

When someone has Type 1 diabetes, their immune system has destroyed insulin-producing cells in the pancreas. Sugar is not processed in the body like it should. This sugar is called *glucose*. It is the body's main energy source. In a person with diabetes, glucose stays in the blood and can't be turned into energy. A person with a lot of glucose in their blood is said to have high blood sugar. Having a lot of glucose in your blood is dangerous and can make you very sick.

Types of Diabetes

There are three main types of diabetes. Type 1 diabetes occurs when a person's pancreas no longer makes insulin. Type 2 diabetes occurs when a person's body makes insulin, but it cannot properly use that insulin. Gestational diabetes occurs in some women when they are pregnant.

A doctor tests a pregnant woman's blood for gestational diabetes.

A woman with Type 2 diabetes checks her blood sugar level.

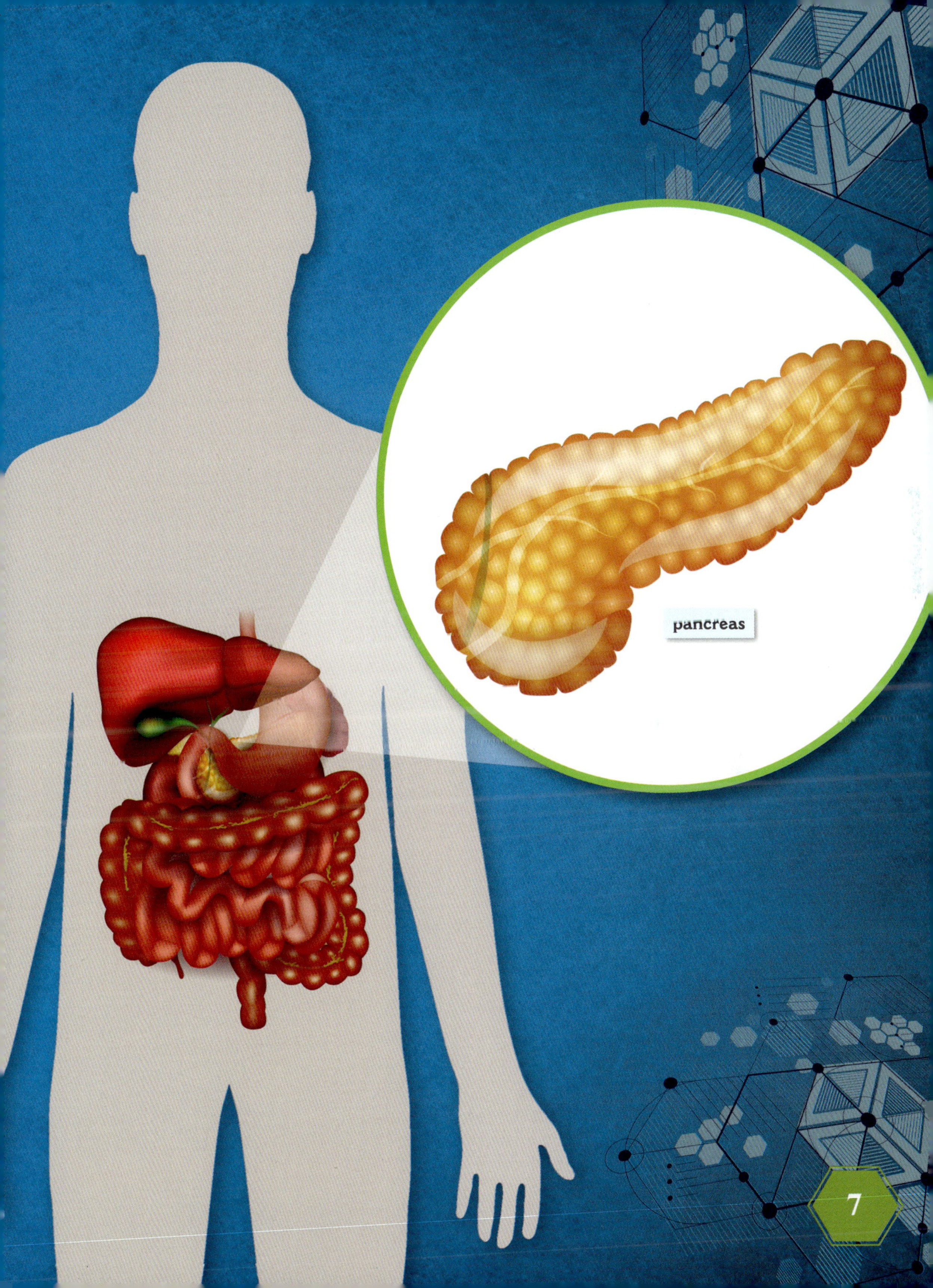
pancreas

What Causes Diabetes?

Researchers are not exactly sure what causes Type 1 diabetes. They are still trying to figure out why this disease affects so many people worldwide. Nearly 3 million people in the United States have Type 1 diabetes. Researchers have some ideas, though. Studies have shown that Type 1 diabetes can be caused by **genetic** factors. People that have certain genes are more likely to have Type 1 diabetes. These genes cause the body to make **antibodies** that destroy cells in the pancreas. Studies have also shown that people who don't have these genes can still develop diabetes from **viruses** or environmental factors.

Regardless of why someone gets Type 1 diabetes, there are three things that are always true:

1. *You cannot "catch" diabetes.* It is not like the common cold. You can't pass it on from one person to the next!

2. *You do not get Type 1 diabetes from eating a lot of sweets.* What a person eats or drinks does not affect whether they get Type 1 diabetes.

3. *Children are not the only ones who get Type 1 diabetes.* Type 1 diabetes used to be called "**juvenile** diabetes" because it mostly affects young children. But people of any age can get this disease.

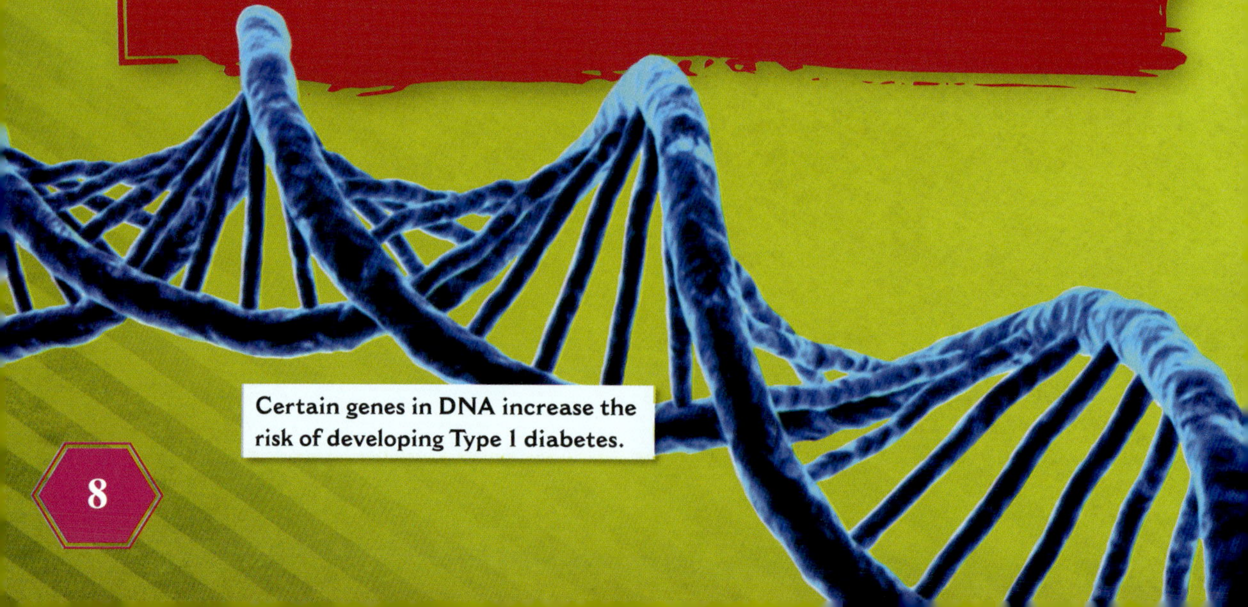

Certain genes in DNA increase the risk of developing Type 1 diabetes.

LET'S EXPLORE MATH

In the United States, about 3,000,000 people have Type 1 diabetes. The total population of the country is about 323,000,000. Label each statement *true* or *false*. Then, change each false statement to make it true.

1. About 3 out of 323 people have Type 1 diabetes.
2. For every 3 people with Type 1 diabetes, there are 320 without it.
3. For every 323 people without Type 1 diabetes, there are 3 with it.
4. The ratio of people with Type 1 diabetes to people without it is 3 to 323.
5. The ratio of people with Type 1 diabetes to people without it is 3 to 320.

This photo, taken with a microscope, shows the pancreas of a person with Type 1 diabetes.

Signs, Symptoms, and Diagnosis

Imagine feeling so tired that it takes all your strength to move your arms and legs. Your mouth is always dry and feels like it's made of cotton. You're always thirsty, yet you can't drink enough to quench your thirst. All the water you drink seems to go right through you, so you feel like the bathroom is now your second home. You're cranky, moody, and you just don't feel right. These are only some of the **symptoms** that people might feel when they have high blood sugar from Type 1 diabetes.

High blood sugar is called **hyperglycemia** (hy-pehr-gly-SEE-mee-ah), and it can be very dangerous to a person's health. This happens when there is too much glucose in the blood and not enough insulin to get the glucose into cells. This can happen if a diabetic person eats without taking enough insulin. High blood sugar can also be caused by illness or stress.

A person's organs may be damaged if their glucose levels are too high for too long. When this happens, toxic acids called **ketones** can develop quickly. This can lead to diabetic **ketoacidosis** (kee-toh-ah-sih-DOH-sihs), a condition that can be life-threatening.

Extreme thirst can be a symptom of Type 1 diabetes.

People with Type 1 diabetes can sometimes feel fatigue.

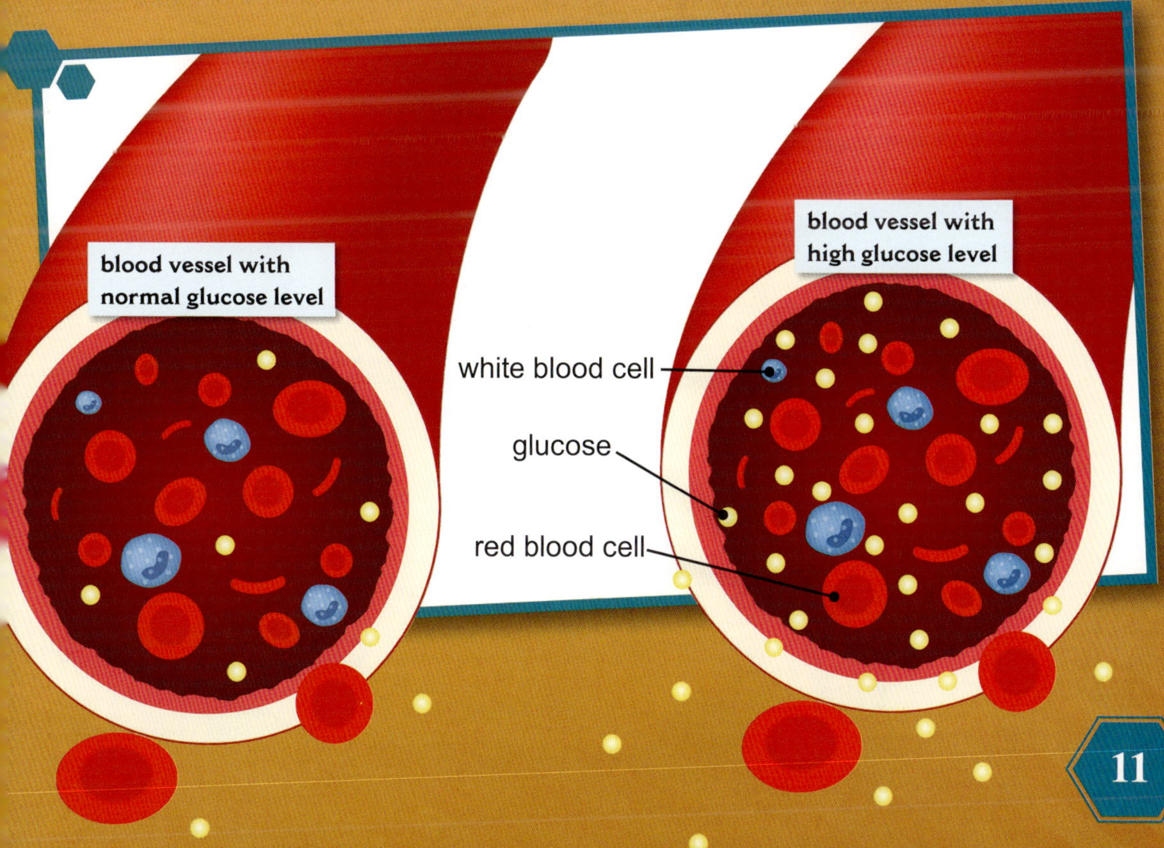

To **diagnose** a person with diabetes, doctors will first look at their symptoms. Along with the symptoms discussed earlier, some people might lose a lot of weight in a short time. They might also have fruity-smelling breath (from ketones). Doctors may order blood tests to get a clear picture of a person's health.

One blood test measures A1C. A1C is a person's average blood sugar level over a three-month period. Doctors may order these blood tests anytime, regardless of when people last ate. Or, doctors may order fasting blood sugar tests. With these tests, people cannot eat or drink for at least eight hours before the test. The results from both types of tests can tell doctors whether a person's blood sugar level is normal or not.

Further testing will distinguish whether a person has Type 1 or Type 2 diabetes. After all this testing, doctors can prescribe a proper treatment plan.

A nurse draws blood from a patient's arm for a blood sugar test.

A lab tech conducts an AIC test.

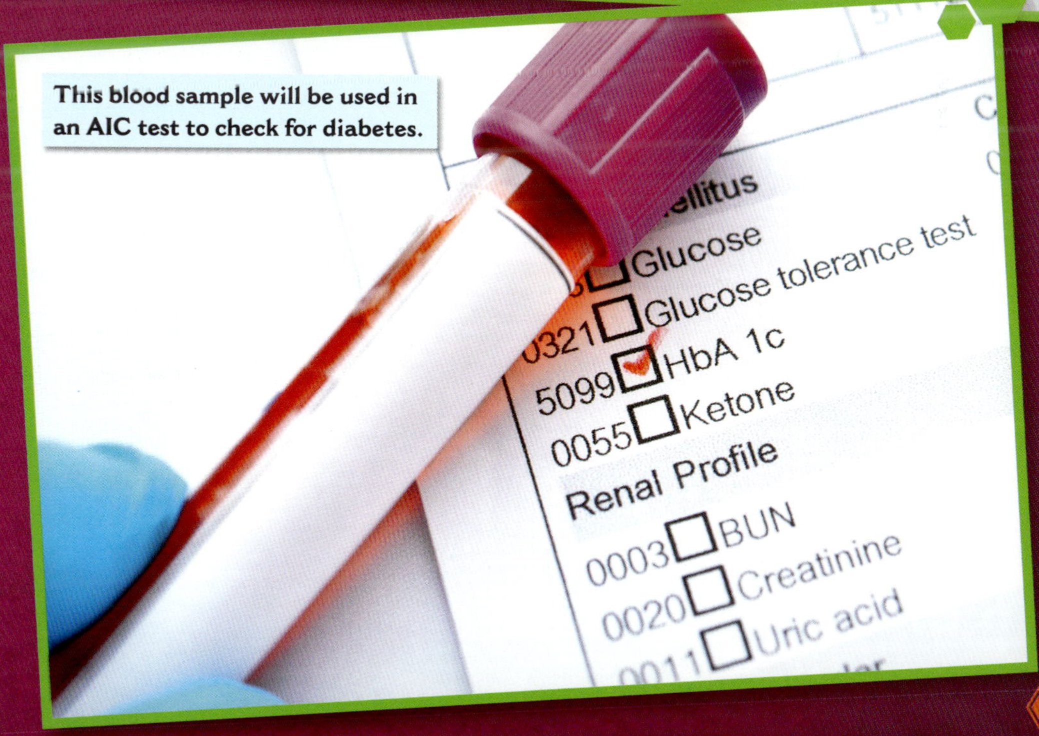

This blood sample will be used in an AIC test to check for diabetes.

Managing the Disease

People with Type 1 diabetes cannot make insulin. So, they must give their bodies the insulin they need. Insulin moves glucose out of the blood and into cells. Then, their cells can use the glucose for energy. People with Type 1 diabetes must take insulin every day, many times a day, for the rest of their lives. Insulin must be injected under the skin with a syringe, an insulin pen, or an insulin pump. It is usually injected in the abdomen, behind the upper arm, or in the thigh.

Some people with diabetes prefer to use insulin pumps. They say that pumps make their lives a little bit easier. These small pumps attach to people's skin where it won't get in the way of day-to-day activities. Pumps deliver insulin through small tubes. People with insulin pumps get insulin all day without having to use needles to inject it. The pump is programmed to deliver different amounts of insulin at different times of the day.

A pump mimics a healthy pancreas because it can be set to deliver more or less insulin when the person needs it. But a person with an insulin pump must still monitor their blood sugar levels. They must tell the pump what to do and when to do it. Oftentimes, this is a guessing game because people's bodies can change quickly.

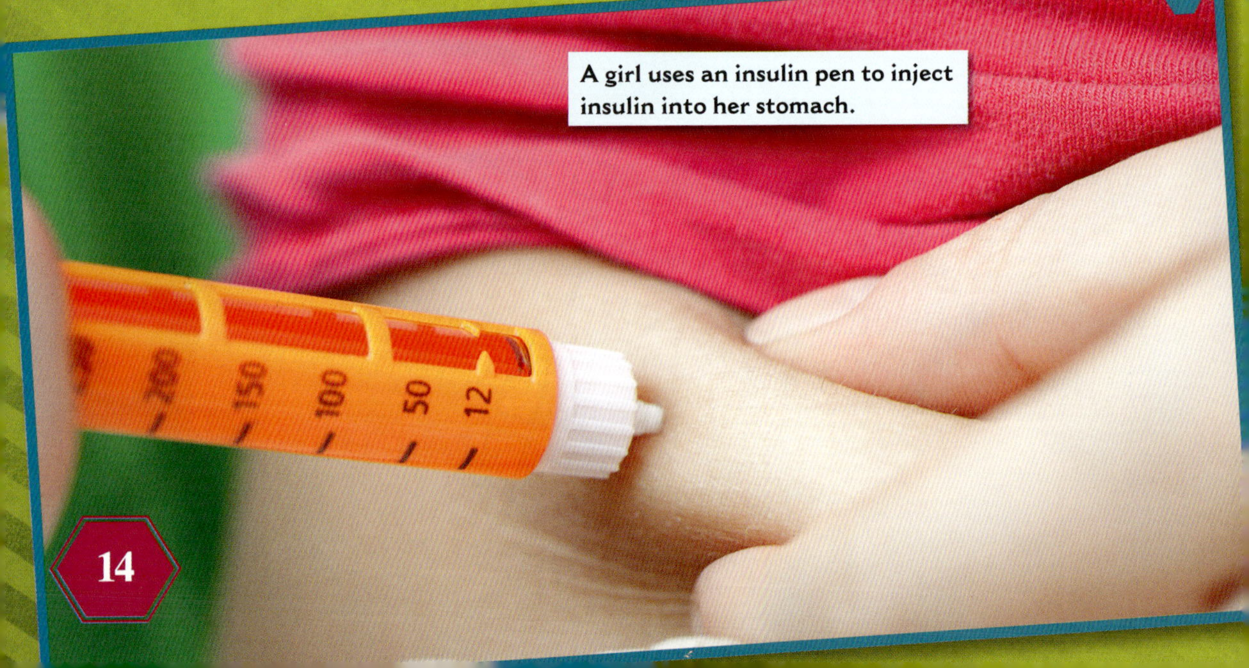

A girl uses an insulin pen to inject insulin into her stomach.

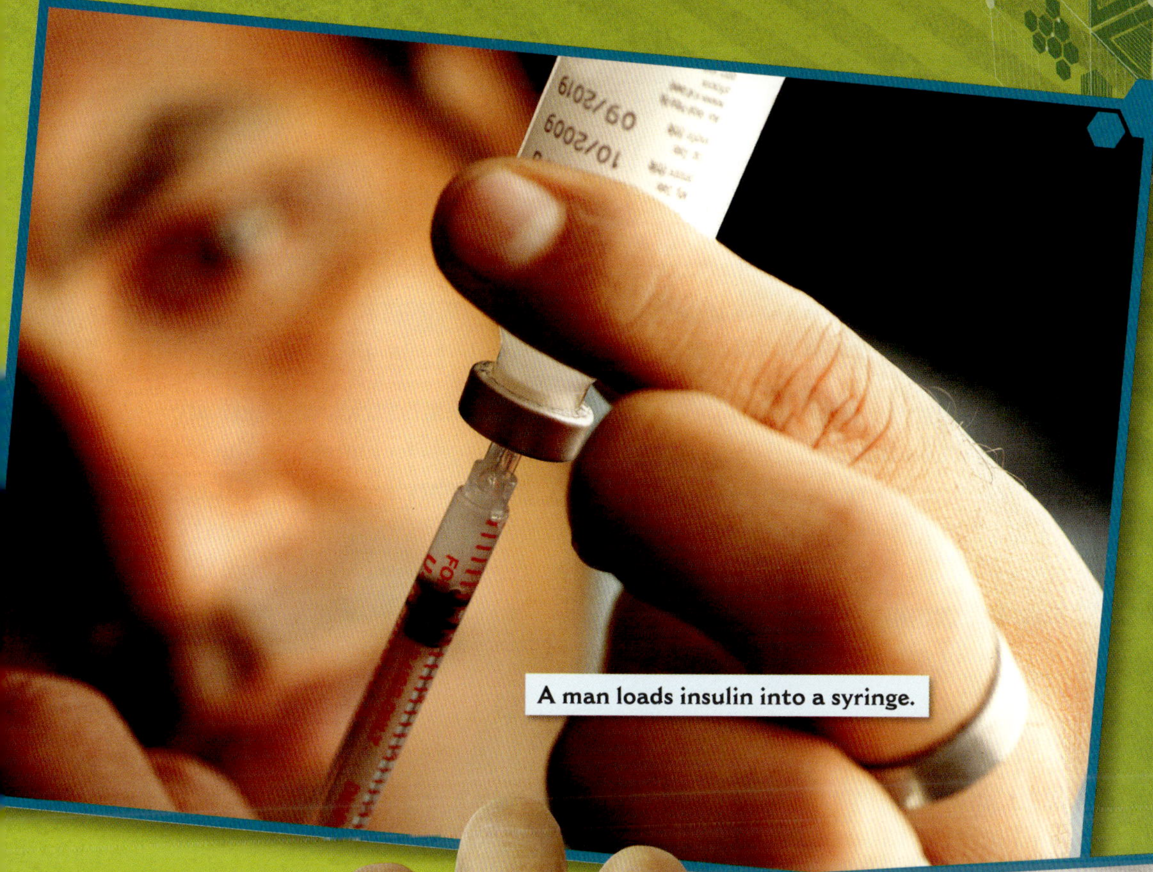

A man loads insulin into a syringe.

a type of insulin pump

Many types of insulin can treat diabetes. Each one acts differently in the body. While some types last a long time, others are fast-acting.

Some types of insulin are taken before eating. The body needs insulin to process food that a person eats into energy. For people with Type 1 diabetes, an injection before or after eating mimics this process.

Choosing the right amount of insulin to take can be tricky. There are many factors that can disrupt the balance that needs to happen in the body. Sometimes, people have too much insulin in their bodies, which will result in low blood sugar. Too much insulin, not enough food, and increased activity can all cause low blood sugar levels. Low blood sugar is called **hypoglycemia**. It can make a person feel shaky, sweaty, dizzy, weak, and confused.

Low blood sugar can happen frequently in someone with diabetes. It can be treated by eating or drinking something sweet, such as candy or fruit juice. Many people with Type 1 diabetes carry snacks with them that will quickly raise their blood sugar if it drops too low.

A woman with hypoglycemia lies down after her blood sugar level drops too low.

LET'S EXPLORE MATH

Suma's doctor recommends that she drink water throughout the day to stay hydrated. She drinks 30 ounces of water in 6 hours. Use the tape diagram to find out more about her plan.

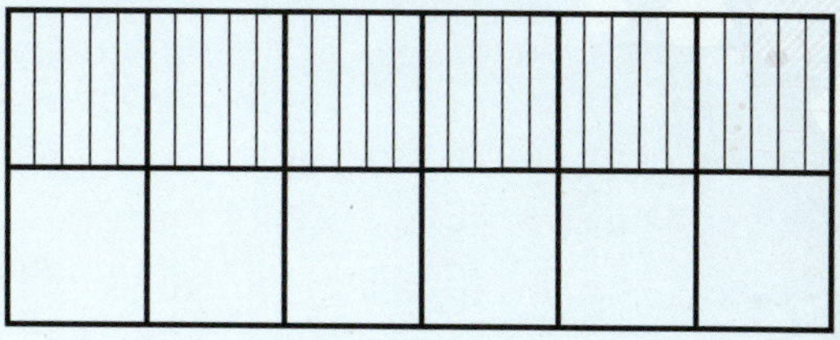

1. How much water does Suma drink in 1 hour?
2. How long does it take her to drink 1 ounce of water?
3. Suma wants to drink water at this same rate while watching her sister's soccer tournament. How can you determine how much water she should bring if the tournament is 8 hours long?

Checks and Balances

People with Type 1 diabetes must check their blood sugar many times during the day. Blood sugar levels can increase and decrease, so people must check often to make the right dosing decisions.

A glucose meter is used to check glucose levels in the blood. There are many types available. One of the most common is a small device with a **lancet**. A person pricks their finger with a lancing device and places a drop of blood on a test strip. The meter then tests the blood and lets the person know their level.

A continuous glucose monitor (CGM) is a more high-tech way to check blood sugar levels. This device uses a sensor that is inserted under the skin, usually in a person's stomach or arm. A CGM measures the glucose in the **interstitial** (ihn-tehr-STIH-shuhl) **fluid** around cells. The CGM checks levels every five minutes, day and night. The sensor sends the information wirelessly to a handheld device or smartphone. If a person's interstitial glucose level drops too low or rises too high, an alarm sounds. CGMs help make the task of monitoring blood sugar a little easier!

A woman pricks her finger with a lancing device.

A girl waves a handheld device over her CGM.

A man inserts a test strip into a glucose meter.

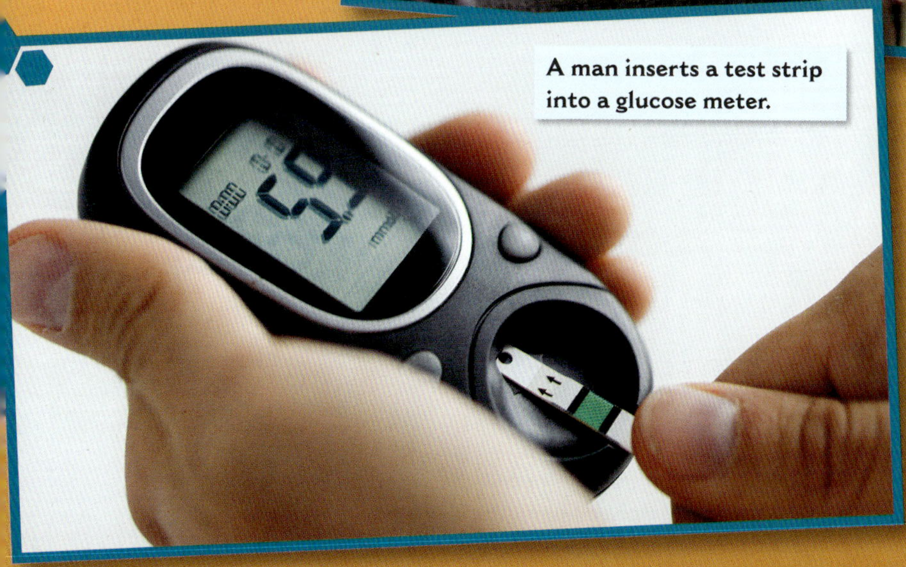

Life with Diabetes

Insulin is used to manage or treat Type 1 diabetes, but it does not cure it. People who are diagnosed with the disease will have it for the rest of their lives. As research into diabetes progresses, many new advances are discovered that help people manage the disease and live long lives.

Eating Right

People with Type 1 diabetes can eat anything they want as long as they give themselves a proper dose of insulin. However, they must think very carefully about the food they eat. This is because food plays a big role in maintaining a healthy blood sugar level. They must know the number of **carbohydrates** (or carbs) in a food before they eat it. Then, they won't eat too many or too few carbs in one day.

Carbs are important **nutrients** that provide our bodies with energy. But carbs are also what make blood sugar rise the most. People with Type 1 diabetes must count carbs to properly dose for the food they eat.

Before or soon after eating, people with Type 1 diabetes will need a dose of fast-acting insulin. This dose is called a *bolus* (BOH-luhs), and it helps their bodies process the sugar in their food. The amount of insulin needed depends on the number of carbs eaten. There is math at every meal!

A girl gives herself an insulin injection before drinking fruit juice.

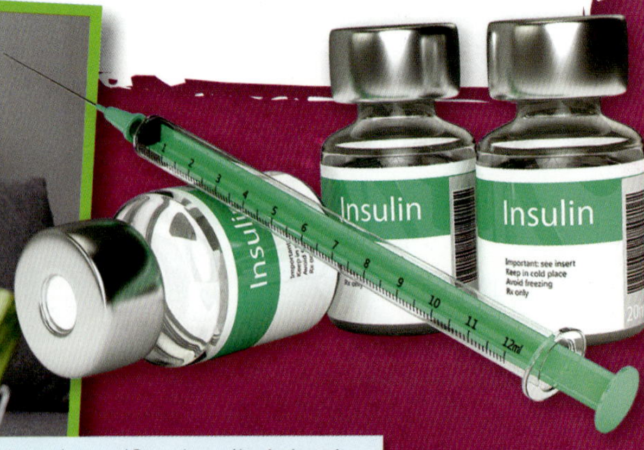

A woman examines a food label while grocery shopping.

LET'S EXPLORE MATH

A person with Type 1 diabetes must carefully read and understand food labels. Use the cereal food label to analyze the carbs.

1. Choose all the correct ratios of serving size to carbs.
   - **A.** For every 56 grams of cereal, there are 42 grams of carbs.
   - **B.** $\frac{4}{3}$
   - **C.** 42:56
   - **D.** $1\frac{1}{3}$ to 1
   - **E.** $\frac{3}{4}$
2. Noah's doctor tells him to take 1 insulin unit for every 15 grams of carbs. Before calculating his exact dose for eating one serving of cereal, Noah estimates. Which estimate most accurately describes Noah's dose?
   - **A.** less than 2 units
   - **B.** exactly 2 units
   - **C.** almost 3 units
   - **D.** more than 3 units

Nutrition Facts
Serving size 56 g Servings per container about 13
Amount per serving
Calories 200 Calories from fat 10
Total Fat 1 g
Saturated Fat 0 g
Trans Fat 0 g
Cholesterol 0 g
Sodium 0 g
Total Carbohydrate 42 g

Staying Active

Exercise is an important part of keeping your body and mind healthy. We all need to move our bodies—even people with Type 1 diabetes. But just as with eating, people with diabetes need to plan ahead. Whether running a race or raking leaves, every little bit of activity affects blood sugar levels.

Doing any form of cardio exercise for a long time, such as running, can make a person's blood sugar level drop. People with Type 1 diabetes must adjust their care based on what they plan to do. They might require a different insulin-to-carb ratio. Or they may need to eat more carbs before exercising. To make sure their levels are within a healthy range, they must check their blood sugar before, during, and after activities. They must also make sure to carry snacks that will raise their blood sugar if it gets too low from exercising.

Type 1 diabetes does not mean an end to a full and active life. It just means a little extra care and planning are required beforehand.

A woman measures her blood sugar level after exercising.

LET'S EXPLORE MATH

Jem's insulin-to-carb ratio is 1:13 for lunch. His insulin-to-carb ratio is 3:32 for dinner. He wants to find out whether the ratios are equivalent.

He starts by drawing a representation of his lunch ratio, using squares to stand for insulin and circles to stand for carbs. Draw his dinner ratio to determine whether the ratios are equivalent.

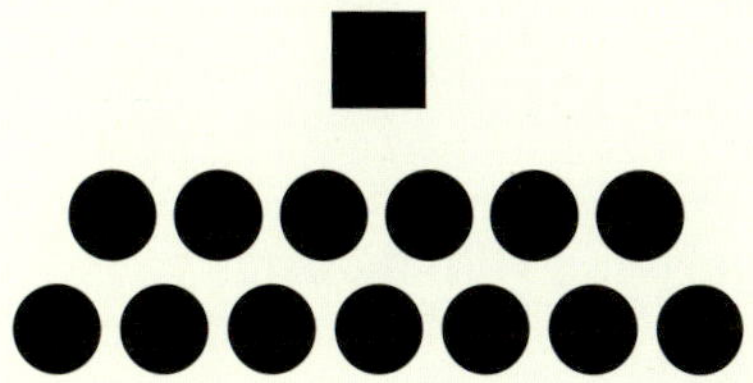

A swimmer measures her blood sugar level while exercising.

A Bright Future

What do Supreme Court Justice Sonia Sotomayor, football quarterback Jay Cutler, and musician/actor Nick Jonas have in common? They all have Type 1 diabetes. Just like everyone with the disease, their days include insulin injections and blood sugar checks. But these people have not let this disease stop them from achieving their dreams. They are all living and thriving with diabetes!

Sonia Sotomayor was diagnosed with Type 1 diabetes at seven years old. When she was a child in the 1960s, people with diabetes were not expected to live long lives. With this in mind, Sotomayor promised herself to make the most of every minute of her life. This promise carried her through college, law school, and all the way to serving as a judge on the highest court in the United States.

In 2013, Sotomayor spoke to eighth, ninth, and tenth graders in Denver, Colorado. Her life with diabetes was one of the topics she talked about. She noted that living with diabetes has given her a positive outlook on life. "It taught me the preciousness of life," she said. "And it taught me that if I wasted any minute of my life, that it would be criminal. That is what kept me going."

Sonia Sotomayor

United States Supreme Court courtroom

Sotomayor dances with kids at a ceremony in New York City where a housing complex was renamed after her.

LET'S EXPLORE MATH

Zahra was recently diagnosed with Type 1 diabetes. Her doctor recommends that she use the "500 rule" to estimate her insulin-to-carb ratio. To use the 500 rule, she divides 500 carbs by the number of insulin units she takes each day. Currently, Zahra takes 40 insulin units daily. Using the 500 rule, she writes her ratio as $\frac{500}{40}$.

1. How many grams of carbs are covered by 1 insulin unit? Use the frames to write the unit rate in three different ways.

   A. For every _______ grams of carbs, Zahra takes 1 insulin unit.

   B. _______ : _______

   C. $\frac{\square}{\square}$

2. How can Zahra use the unit rate to determine the number of insulin units she must take before a meal?

Jay Cutler found out he had Type 1 diabetes when he was 24. At the time, he was a quarterback for the Denver Broncos. He was first told that the symptoms he was feeling were from the stress of playing football.

Once Cutler knew he had diabetes, he spent the summer trying to find what worked for him. He tried different insulins, tracked his blood sugar levels, and changed his diet. Despite this major life change, he continued playing in the National Football League®.

Musician and actor Nick Jonas didn't let Type 1 diabetes stop him from becoming a star. Jonas was 13 years old when he found out he had diabetes. He quickly learned all he could about the disease. He wanted to manage his diabetes without missing a beat. Jonas later cofounded Beyond Type 1, an organization that raises money and awareness for people with Type 1 diabetes.

Researchers around the world are working to find a cure for Type 1 diabetes. They are also looking for ways to make the lives of people with the disease a little easier. In the future, there may be even more advanced devices and scientific discoveries. In the meantime, with good medical care and support from friends and family, people with Type 1 diabetes can and do live long, healthy, and active lives.

Jay Cutler takes the snap during a game.

Nick Jonas

LET'S EXPLORE MATH

Funda's doctor recommends that before her meals, she take 1 insulin unit for every 24 grams of carbs. Her dad packs her lunch with these food items:

- apple 25 g carbs
- hummus bagel sandwich 70 g carbs
- dark chocolate candy bar 25 g carbs

1. Write Funda's insulin-to-carb recommendation as a ratio. Label the values.
2. How many insulin units does the school nurse give Funda before she eats her lunch? Use words, numbers, or pictures to prove your solution.

Problem Solving

World Diabetes Day is celebrated every year on November 14. The goal of the day is to increase diabetes awareness. Imagine that you are a member of your school's wellness club. The club is going to design posters in honor of World Diabetes Day to increase diabetes understanding among students. Libby, the president of the club, tells members to feature ratios on their posters to make the statistics stand out. Use the data to analyze Libby's poster, and create your own eye-catching design.

1. Libby makes a poster.

   a. Which data did Libby use to calculate the ratio?

   b. Why do you think Libby used "about 1 out of 5" instead of numbers from the table?

2. Design your own poster to increase diabetes awareness. Include at least two different ratios. Remember to add graphics that will draw people's attention. On the back of your poster, explain what the ratios mean and show the work you did to write them.

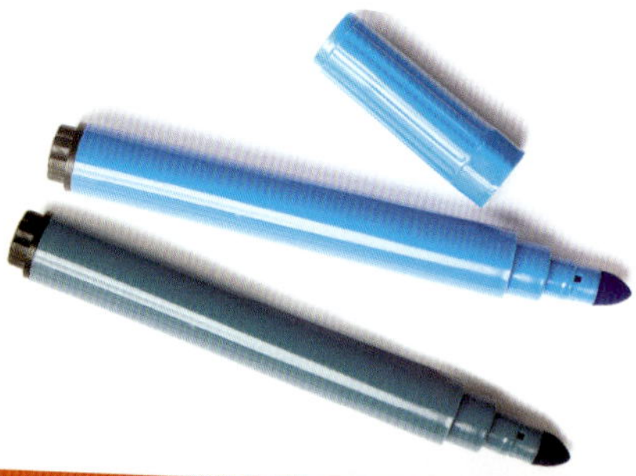

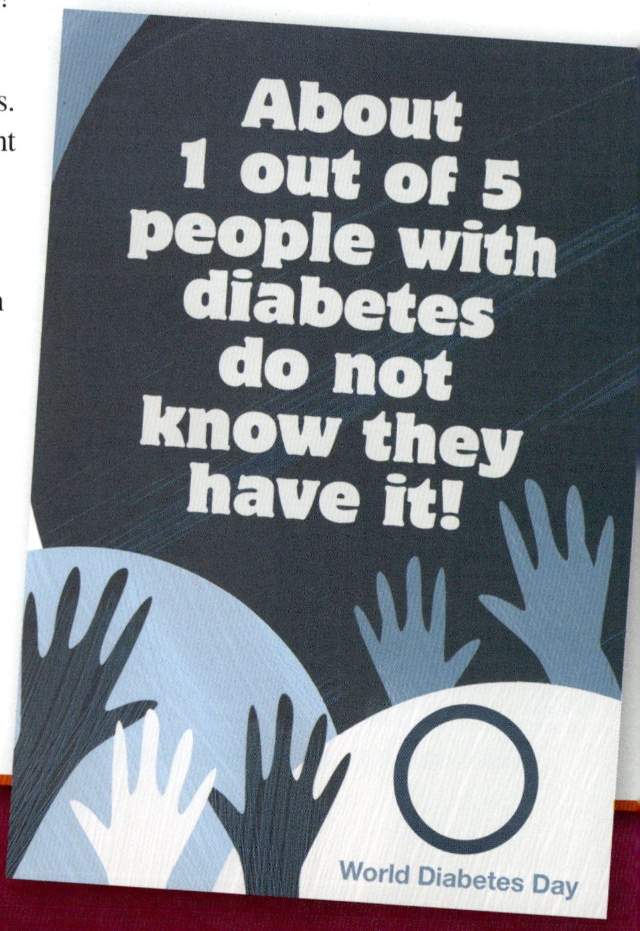

Estimated Number of Adults in the United States with Type 1 and Type 2 Diabetes

Characteristic	Number of People with Diagnosed Diabetes	Number of People with Undiagnosed Diabetes
Age (years)		
18–44	3,000,000	1,600,000
45–64	10,700,000	3,600,000
65 and over	9,900,000	2,100,000
Gender		
Women	11,700,000	3,100,000
Men	11,300,000	4,000,000

(Note: Numbers are estimates, which is why totals are different.)

Glossary

antibodies—substances made by the body to fight diseases

autoimmune disease—a condition that causes a person's immune system to mistakenly attack healthy cells and organs

carbohydrates—substances found in certain foods that provide bodies with energy

diagnose—to identify a disease by examining someone

genetic—relating to genes, which are physical or mental traits passed down from parents

hormone—a natural substance in the body that helps cells and organs do what they need to

hyperglycemia—when the level of glucose in the blood is higher than it should be

hypoglycemia—when the level of glucose in the blood is lower than it should be

insulin—a hormone in the body that turns sugar into energy

interstitial fluid—liquid in the body that surrounds cells

juvenile—relating to people who are too young to be considered adults

ketoacidosis—a life-threatening condition that can happen in people with diabetes in which acids build up in the bloodstream

ketones—chemicals that show up in blood and urine when fats are broken down for energy

lancet—a sharp tool used for cutting the skin

nutrients—substances people need to live and grow

pancreas—a large gland in the body that makes insulin and helps the body process food

symptoms—changes in the body that may indicate the presence of a disease

viruses—certain types of illnesses or diseases

Index

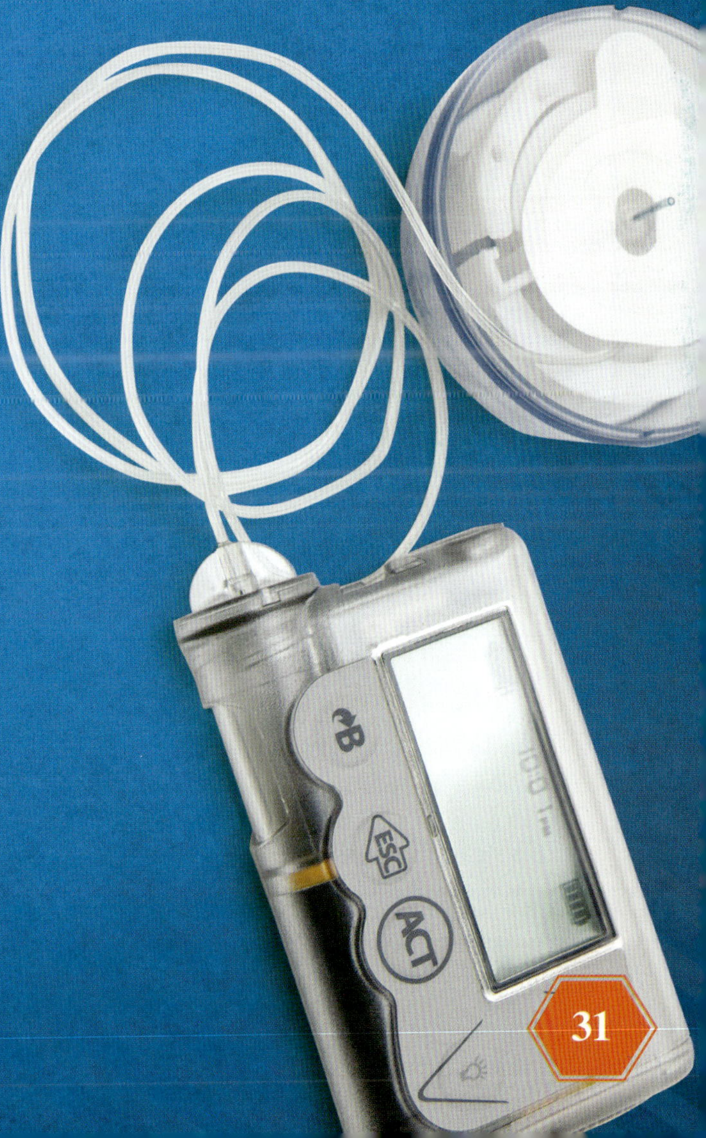

Answer Key

Let's Explore Math

page 5

1. A, D
2. This means 3 students out of 12 total students visited the nurse to have their blood sugar levels checked.

page 9

1. true
2. true
3. false; For every 320 people without Type 1 diabetes, there are 3 with it.
4. false; The ratio of people with Type 1 diabetes to people without it is 3 to 320.
5. true

page 17

1. 5 oz.
2. $\frac{1}{5}$ hour, or 12 minutes
3. Suma needs 5 oz. per hour for 8 hours ($5 \times 8 = 40$).

page 21

1. A, B, D
2. C

page 23

The ratios are not equivalent. If the ratios were equivalent, Jem's current ratio would be 3:39, not 3:32. Representations should show 3 squares and 39 circles.

page 25

1. **a.** $12\frac{1}{2}$

   b. $12\frac{1}{2}$:1

   c. $\frac{12\frac{1}{2}}{1}$
2. Zahra can divide the number of carbs in the meal by $12\frac{1}{2}$.

page 27

1. 1:24; 1 insulin unit and 24 g of carbs
2. 5 insulin units; $24 \times 5 = 120$ or $120 \div 24 = 5$

Problem Solving

1. **a.** 7,100,000–7,300,000 people with undiagnosed diabetes and 30,100,000–30,900,000 total people with diagnosed and undiagnosed diabetes

   b. simplified, rounded numbers are easier to read on posters
2. Posters should include graphics, at least two different ratios, and work to prove reasonableness.